A LOOK AT MONEY MATTERS

DEBT

BY ROSIE BANKS

CRASHCOURSE

Gareth Stevens
PUBLISHING

Please visit our website, www.garethstevens.com. For a free color catalog of all our high-quality books, call toll free 1-800-542-2595 or fax 1-877-542-2596.

Library of Congress Cataloging-in-Publication Data

Names: Banks, Rosie, 1978- author.
Title: Debt / Rosie Banks.
Description: New York : Gareth Stevens Publishing, [2024] | Series: A look at money matters | Includes bibliographical references and index.
Identifiers: LCCN 2023029123 (print) | LCCN 2023029124 (ebook) | ISBN 9781538292310 (library binding) | ISBN 9781538292303 (paperback) | ISBN 9781538292327 (ebook)
Subjects: LCSH: Debt--Juvenile literature. | Loans--Juvenile literature. | Money--Juvenile literature.
Classification: LCC HG3755 .B34 2024 (print) | LCC HG3755 (ebook) | DDC 332.024/02--dc23/eng/20230622
LC record available at https://lccn.loc.gov/2023029123
LC ebook record available at https://lccn.loc.gov/2023029124

First Edition

Published in 2024 by
Gareth Stevens Publishing
2544 Clinton Street
Buffalo, NY 14224

Designer: Leslie Taylor
Editor: Therese Shea

Photo credits: Cover (wallet) Khrystyna Sun/Shutterstock.com; cover & series art (background) creativenv/Shutterstock.com; series art (falling coins) Abscent Vector/Shutterstock.com, (moneybag) VectorArtist7/Shutterstock.com; p. 5 Volurol/Shutterstock.com; p. 7 Billion Photos/Shutterstock.com; p. 9 Lane V. Erickson/iStockphoto.com; p. 11 alexskopje/Shutterstock.com; p. 13 Nattakorn_Maneerat/Shutterstock.com; p. 15 4 PM production/Shutterstock.com; p. 17 SB Arts Media/Shutterstock.com; p. 19 Andy Dean Photography/Shutterstock.com; p. 21 NicoElNino/Shutterstock.com; p. 23 Everett Collection/Shutterstock.com; p. 25 Paul Brady Photography/Shutterstock.com; p. 27 Jason Raff/Shutterstock.com; p. 29 Prostock-studio/Shutterstock.com.

Printed in the United States of America

CONTENTS

Words in the glossary appear in **bold** type the first time they are used in the text.

MONEY OWED

Have you ever borrowed money? Maybe you wanted a toy that cost a bit more money than you had. So you borrowed money from someone to buy it. You then **owed** that person money. That owed money is called debt.

MAKE THE GRADE

People who owe money are said to be "in debt."

Debt is a big part of life for many people. Not all debt is bad. Some is necessary. Some things people need cost a lot of money. It's not always possible to save up enough money when these things are needed.

MAKE THE GRADE

People often take on debt when they buy cars and houses. These things can be expensive, or costly.

INTEREST MEANS MORE

People often borrow money from a bank or company. They sign many papers promising to pay back the borrowed money, called a loan. There's a cost to borrow this money. It's called interest. The amount charged is called the **interest rate**.

MAKE THE GRADE

When people pay back the loaned money, they end up paying more. They pay back the whole amount they borrowed and the interest.

An interest rate is a **percentage** of the borrowed amount. How interest works depends on the agreement. If you borrowed $1,000 with a 5% simple interest rate for one year, you'll pay back $1,050. A kind of interest called compound interest means even more money is owed.

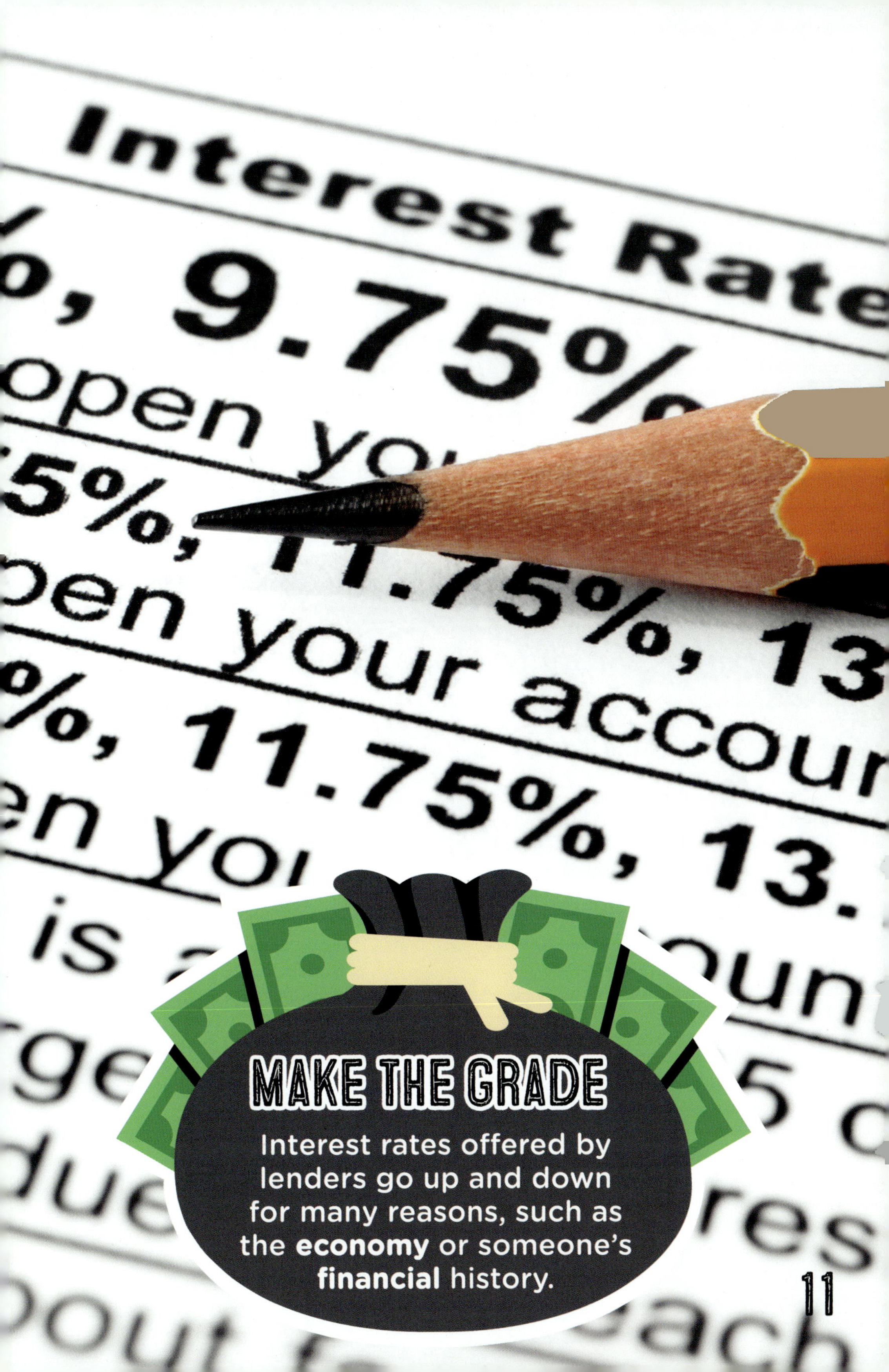

MAKE THE GRADE

Interest rates offered by lenders go up and down for many reasons, such as the **economy** or someone's **financial** history.

LOTS OF LOANS

Loans come in many forms. Car loans are used to buy cars and trucks. Student loans are used to pay for school. Mortgages are loans to buy homes and land. A credit card is also a way to borrow money. All these loans charge interest.

MAKE THE GRADE

Credit cards are like small loans. But if you pay off the amount borrowed each month, no interest is charged. If you don't, you'll pay interest.

GOOD OR BAD?

Good debt is borrowed for needed things, such as a home. Good debt is also debt you can pay back. Bad debt is money spent on things that you can live without. Bad debt is also debt that you can't pay back as promised.

MAKE THE GRADE

Things that rise in value, such as a house, can be good debt. Things that will help you make money, such as loans for school, are too. Your school studies can help you get a job.

IF YOU DON'T PAY...

All loans are agreements. Borrowers agree to pay back the money in a certain way. What happens if they don't make a payment on time? That should be in the agreement. It may say borrowers need to pay the payment plus a late fee.

MAKE THE GRADE

If a loan isn't paid back on time, a person's debt can grow much larger.

If you miss making several payments in a row, the loan may go into **default.** If a car loan goes into default, the lender can take the car. A mortgage in default can mean a borrower loses their home. This is called foreclosure.

MAKE THE GRADE

Debt can be sold to a person or company too. They then "own" the debt and can collect the money.

CREDIT SCORES

Another reason people should pay back loans on time is their credit score. A credit score is a number that tells lenders how likely a borrower is to pay back a loan. Most credit scores are between 300 (low) and 850 (high).

MAKE THE GRADE

Missed payments and loan defaults affect a credit score. A lender may not lend money to someone with a low credit score.

NATIONAL DEBT

Countries have debt too! Sometimes they need to borrow money to pay for all the **programs** and services people need. For example, the U.S. national debt in June 2023 was about $23 **trillion** and Canada's national debt was about 1.2 trillion Canadian dollars.

MAKE THE GRADE

The U.S national debt began when the country did! The new United States borrowed money to fight the American Revolution and win freedom from Britain.

Countries make **budgets** to plan how they will spend **revenue** such as taxes. However, sometimes they still spend more than they take in. This difference between revenue that comes in and overspending is called a deficit.

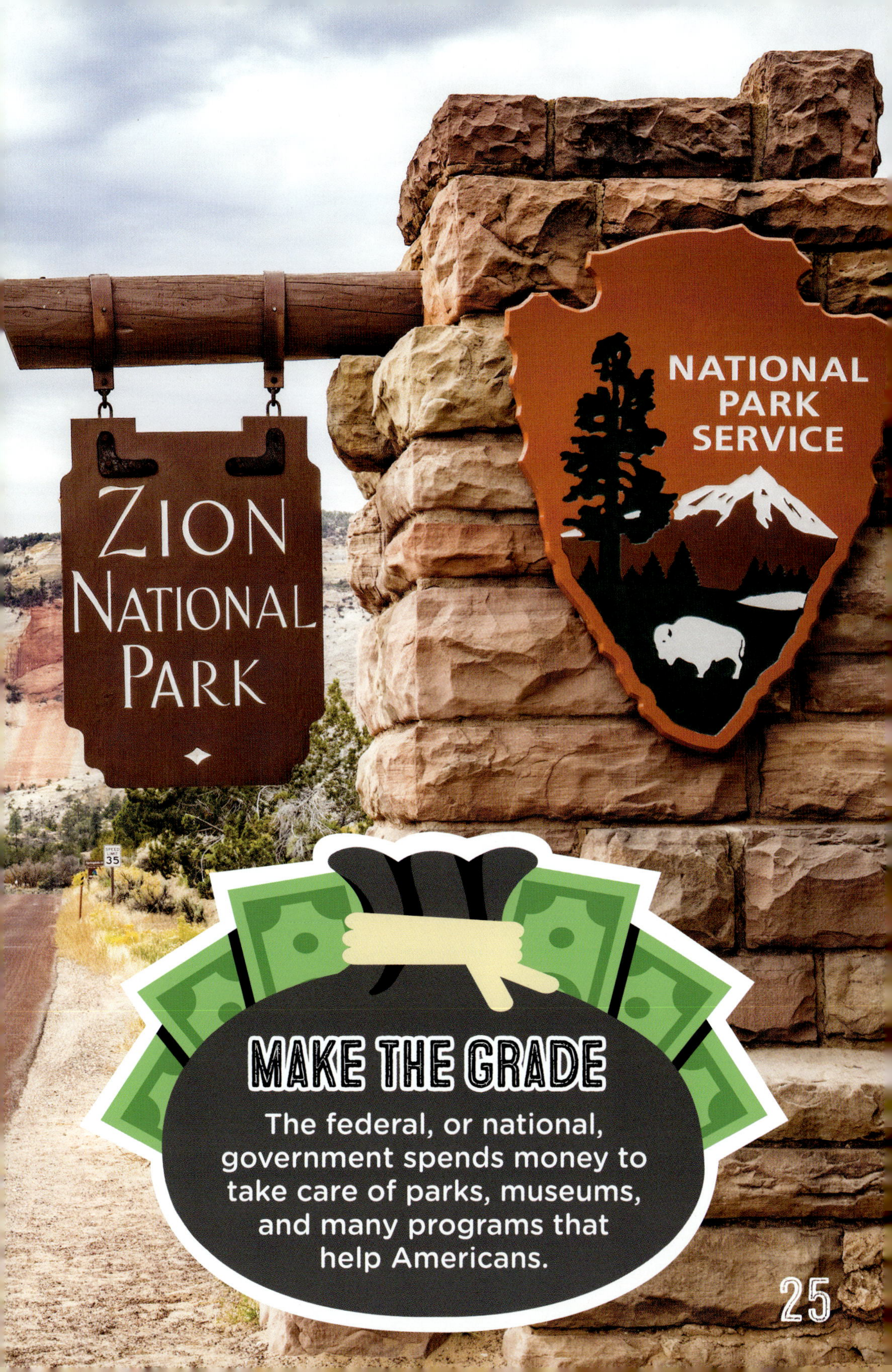

MAKE THE GRADE

The federal, or national, government spends money to take care of parks, museums, and many programs that help Americans.

Who does the U.S. government borrow from? Anyone it can! People, businesses, and other governments can buy government **securities**, such as savings **bonds**. When people buy these, they're loaning money to the government. The government promises to pay them back plus interest.

MAKE THE GRADE

The U.S. government has never defaulted on its debts.

LEARN TO BUDGET!

All debt isn't bad. What *is* bad is not paying debts. That can get people in financial trouble. A budget is important for everyone. Budgets help us plan how to spend money, pay debts, and save up for fun things too!

MAKE THE GRADE

Many people suggest the 50/30/20 budget. That means 50 percent of your **income** is for needs, 30 percent is for wants, and 20 percent is for savings or paying off debt.

GOOD DEBT VS. BAD DEBT

Good Debt

- has value in the future
- helps you grow your money
- has a lower interest rate

Examples:

- house
- business
- used car to get to work

Bad Debt

- loses value right away
- doesn't help you make money
- has a higher interest rate

Examples:

- restaurant dinners
- credit card debt
- expensive car

GLOSSARY

bond: A paper that shows a government or company promises to pay back an amount of money that it has borrowed with interest.

budget: A plan used to figure out how money will be spent.

default: The failure to pay a debt.

economy: The money made in an area and how it is made.

financial: Having to do with money.

income: Money earned.

interest rate: The amount a lender charges a borrower, which is a percentage of the amount loaned.

owe: To need to repay money to someone.

percentage: A number that is expressed as a part of 100, often using the % symbol after it.

program: A set of activities to accomplish something.

revenue: The money collected by the government for use.

security: A debt obligation, or duty, backed by the government.

trillion: The number 1,000,000,000,000.

FOR MORE INFORMATION

BOOKS

Burling, Alexis. *Managing Debt.* Minneapolis, MN: Essential Library, 2020.

Kallen, Stuart A. *Managing Credit and Debt.* San Diego, CA: ReferencePoint Press, 2021.

WEBSITE

Interest: An Introduction

www.mathsisfun.com/money/interest.html

Learn how to figure out interest owed on money borrowed.

Publisher's note to educators and parents: Our editors have carefully reviewed these websites to ensure that they are suitable for students. Many websites change frequently, however, and we cannot guarantee that a site's future contents will continue to meet our high standards of quality and educational value. Be advised that students should be closely supervised whenever they access the internet.

INDEX